Diary of Steve the Noob 2

Steve the Noob

Thank You

Thank you for picking up a copy of my book. I spent many hours putting this book together, so I hope that you will enjoy reading it. As a Minecraft player, it brings me great joy to be able to share my stories with you. The game is fun and entertaining, and surprisingly, writing about it can be almost just as fun. Once you are done reading this book, if you enjoyed it, please take a moment to leave a review. It will help other people discover this book. If after reading it, you realize that you hate it with such passion, please feel free to leave me a review anyway. I enjoy reading what people think about my books and writing style. I hope that many people will like this book and encourage me to keep writing. Thanks in advance.

Special thanks to readers of my previous books. Thank you for taking the time to leave a review. I appreciate it so much; your support means so much to me. I will continue to keep writing and will try to provide the highest quality of unofficial Minecraft books. Thank you for your support.

4/8/2017

Thanks for the support, everyone! Because of you all, this series has grown up to 24 books and still going strong! Book 25 should be out around the 19th of April. I updated book 2 with the list of my favorite readers and reviewers. I also changed the cover to match the rest of the series.

Check Out My Author Page
Steve the Noob

My Other Books
Diary of Steve the Noob
Herobrine the Anti-Hero

Monday

I have been walking through these great, flat plains for hours now.

There was not a soul in sight.

I was starting to feel a bit lonely, and the only thing to keep my company was the haunting thoughts of my previous failure.

You see, a few days ago, I left my adopted town because I had failed to defend the villagers from an invasion of mobs.

The mobs completely wiped out all my friends in the village, and I was the only survivor. I left because I was ashamed and felt guilty because I had failed them; also, I was afraid of ghosts.

The town had become an eerily quiet place, a hollow shell of its former self. It was time to move on.

Here I am today, traveling through this area, I don't know what I'll find, but all I know is that I must find a way to end this nightly plague of monsters.

But who knows?

Maybe the monsters come out at night only in that particular area, or is this a widespread problem? I guess I'll find out later tonight.

As I wandered, I got really hungry. I would have packed some food for the journey, but during the raid of the previous village, all the crops burned down.

I came across some chickens and immediately pursued them with my wooden sword. They didn't put up a fight, but they did run all over the place.

I was able to gather some raw chicken meat and feathers from them. I didn't have access to a fire, nor did I know how to start a fire, so my only choice for the chicken meat was to eat it raw.

That didn't sound really appealing, so I attempted to build a fire. I remembered something about rubbing two sticks together extremely fast would cause high friction and start a fire, so I took two wooden sticks and placed them in my crafting kit.

I tried all sorts of different arrangements, but nothing produced a campfire kit, or fire starting kit. After about an hour, I just gave up and decided to eat the chicken meat raw.

The meat was kind of slimy and gooey; it didn't smell very good. But I was close to starving, so I just closed my eyes and took big bites. It was very chewy and tasted kind of funny.

Gulp.

I did my best to swallow it down. It was okay, I guess, but something just felt off.

I continued to wander the great plains, but about an hour later, my stomach felt really weird. It was like a bubbling, churning sensation at first, but later, it started to really hurt.

It turned out I got food poisoning from consuming raw chicken. I had to go poo like every 20 minutes.

Oh my goodness, it was a terrible ordeal.

There was no toilet and no soft, luxurious double-ply toilet paper for me to use. There were no trees or bushes where I could hide and do my business, but I guess that's okay because there was no one around.

So, I dug a hole in the dirt and did my business there.

Every 20 minutes….

This continued throughout the day, and before I knew it, it was nightfall. There I was, squatting over a hole in the dirt, when all of a sudden an arrow struck me in the butt!

"OW! What the heck? Who did that?!" I yelled.

There was no answer.

Another arrow whizzed past me.

"Whoa! Whoa! Time out! I'm friendly!" I screamed as I pulled up my pants and stood up.

I heard the clattering of bones. It was a skeleton archer! He had caught me with my pants around my ankles.

I wasn't feeling well, so instead of fighting him, I decided to make a run for it.

Good thing he was slow and I was able to outrun him, but I took another two arrows in my back before I got out of range.

As it turns out, I guess this monster problem is widespread. The night was already here, and the mobs were starting to spawn. I had nowhere to run or hide, and I was sick, weak, and injured.

I thought about laying down and playing dead, maybe that would trick them, but it was too risky.

Then I had an idea.

I'll just dig a big hole and hide myself in it. At least I will be out of sight, and they won't attack what they can't see, I thought.

I've been digging holes all day, so that's my new solution to everything.

So, I dug myself a pillar dirt shelter. It was a quick and easy job, three blocks down and that's it.

I hopped in and prayed nothing would find me. Throughout the night, I could hear the clonking of skeleton bones and moans of brain-hungry zombies.

It kept me up all night, but there were short moments where I fell asleep standing up, leaning against the dirt. This wasn't the greatest shelter, but I guess it was better than being eaten alive.

Tuesday

I awoke the next morning to the sounds of cows. I guess a herd of cows must have roamed over to my location over the night. As I was trying to climb out of my dirt pillar, a cow came over and blocked my way out.

"Shoo! You stupid cow, get out of my way!" I shouted crankily.

"MoOooOOooo…" replied the cow.

Then the cow proceeded to poo into the hole where I was in.

"ARGGGH!!! NOOO!"

I was tired, hungry, cranky, and now stinky, too?! Oh, heck no! That was the last straw.

I drew out my wooden sword and used my special sword technique: Rising Blade.

I flew out of the hole and stabbed that stupid cow multiple times in the process. I chased down the cow that defiled me and made burgers out of it.

Because I was so furious, I destroyed the entire cow herd by using my other sword technique: Whirlwind Strike.

After the dust had settled and I had calmed down, I found about a dozen leather and beef pieces scattered all over the place.

I guess that was a good side effect of my rage mode. Though, in the process I may have accidently slain a few baby cows. I felt kind of bad, but whatever.

I continued walking in the same direction and off in the distance, I saw a village. I was super excited because I was lonely and missed civilization. Also, I knew they would have food, water, and shelter there.

I arrived in the new village in the afternoon. It was a bit bigger than the previous village. There were a couple of different buildings that I didn't recognize like one that had a lava pit.

I wandered the village a little bit and was greeted by the mayor.

"Hello, weary traveler. Welcome to our humble village. We are peaceful villagers and don't want any trouble," said the mayor.

"Hello, sir. My name is Steve the noob, and I am just a weary traveler that needs a place to stay and recover from my injuries and illness," I replied.

"I see. Nice to meet you, Steve. As long as you are not a trouble maker, you may stay in our village."

The mayor showed me around and introduced me to some villagers.

"Here, we have our forge and blacksmith shop. Because our village is a bit bigger than most, we had to create this building. You may use the furnace to cook food and smelt ores."

"Ah! That would be most useful! I had to eat raw chicken yesterday, and it gave me mad diarrhea. I was pooping all over the place, but thankfully, the illness is wearing off," I said.

The mayor shook his head. "Ahem. Too much information, my friend. Too…much…information…"

I laughed.

The mayor quickly changed the topic. "Steve, allow me to introduce to you Bob the blacksmith."

"Hi, if you need any tools, I can trade you an iron shovel for a few emeralds," said Bob to me.

"Thanks! I could use that shovel to dig myself a new home."

"Dig yourself a new home?" he asked curiously.

"Yeah, I discovered that digging a dirt shelter is an effective way to hide against the monsters at night."

Bob laughs. "Boy, forget your dirt hole and come stay with me for a while until you can properly stand on your feet."

"Really? That is a generous offer, thank you. I will repay your kindness one day."

"It is no problem, just pull your own weight around this village is all that I ask."

"Thank you. I will, I promise."

Nighttime was almost upon us now, so I followed Bob to his house. It was a simple wooden building with two bedrooms.

"Here we are. There's your bedroom. Might I suggest one thing, take a shower when you can; you smell like cow poo," Bob said as he laughed.

"Oh, that's right! I, uh, stepped in some cow poo earlier today…" I replied hesitatingly.

"Well, that explains the smell," he replied with a smirk, "I'll lay out some clothes for you to change into and prepare some food."

After taking a shower, I joined Bob for dinner. Zombies were already lined up at our door.

"Oh, don't worry about those guys. I built an iron door to keep the zombies out, so that I could sleep peacefully at night," Bob said proudly.

"That was a great idea."

During dinner, I told Bob about myself, my previous village, and my quest to eliminate the monsters that spawn nightly.

"That is quite a noble goal," he said. "So, do you plan on defending this village as well?"

"Yes, I intend to, since you guys generously took me in with open arms. I will do my best to protect this town."

"Are you planning to build a sturdier wall this time around?"

"I was thinking instead of a wall, I could dig a trench around the village. Mobs would fall in the trench and get stuck. I'll get started on digging right away tomorrow morning."

"That sounds like a pretty good idea. It sucks hiding indoors all the time. With your trench, we might be able to go outside at night. I'll tell you what, I'm gonna give you my iron shovel, so that you can complete your task faster."

"Really? That item would be extremely useful."

"Yeah, you bet. You can dig faster and longer with this tool," Bob said as he handed me the iron shovel.

The item was surprisingly heavy. "Thank you so much, Bob," I said happily, "I will put it to good use."

"I know you will. I know you will…"

Wednesday

I woke up the next morning ready to get to work. With my new iron shovel, this should be a cakewalk. I wanted to recruit some of the villagers to help me dig, but I didn't really know anyone yet.

Bob helped me get started at first, but then he had to go run the blacksmith.

It was a monumental job, but it had to be done. I projected that this trench was going to take a few days to become completed.

Some villagers saw me digging hard and came by to see what's up. Some of them rolled up their sleeves and helped me out.

Unfortunately, they didn't have access to any tools, so they had to dig with their hands and that took forever.

I was able to dig something like three times faster because I had the iron shovel. I thought about taking a break to build some shovels out of wood and stone, but there were no extra materials laying around in this great, flat land.

A villager named Cindy approached me. "I think it is wonderful what you are doing for the village," she said shyly.

"It is my pleasure to help in whatever way I can," I replied.

"I would help you dig this trench, but I have to go tend the family farm."

"Oh, it is okay, we have plenty of hands here."

She smiled. "I'm gonna go off to work now, but before I leave I wanted to give you a suggestion for your trench."

"Yeah, sure, what is it?"

"The monsters that spawn every night are afraid of fire. I'm not sure if they are actually afraid of getting burned, or they are afraid of the light from the fire, maybe it is both. But either way, they tend to avoid an area if there is a torch nearby," she explained, "this is the reason why we always keep torches close to our homes."

"Oohhhh, that makes a lot of sense. So, I should go place more torches around the village and the trench."

"You're a sharp one," she said, "I'll see you later, Steve."

As I watched her watch away, I thought to myself, *where am I going to find more torches or materials to craft torches?*

Then an idea occurred to me. I knew exactly where I could find a ton of materials that no one was using. The place with a vast wealth of torches, wood, stone, and other materials is my previous adopted village, the ghost town.

I didn't really want to return there, not after leaving so recently. But in order to defend this village, I must travel back to that location.

We continued to dig until around 6pm. Then it was time to get home and go into hiding. I thanked everyone for their hard work and told them about my plan for gathering torches and materials to build shovels. Everyone decided to take a break until I returned from my trip.

I met up with Bob that night and had dinner. We ate rabbit stew with steaks on the side. Bob was a marvelous cook.

"My goodness, this is delicious. Is this a secret recipe?" I asked.

Bob laughed. "Oh, no. It is just your typical stew that I made using the furnace at work," he said modestly.

"Can you teach me to make this? I would love to learn."

"Of course, bud. All you need is rabbit meat, a baked potato, a carrot, and a mushroom. When you gather those items, I will help you prepare it. I also know a bunch of other recipes too, if you are interested."

Later on, I found out that Bob sometimes doubled as the village assistant chef. It all made sense. I told Bob about my plan for tomorrow.

"Thank you for your hospitality, Bob. When I return from the ghost town, I'd like to build a house next to yours, so that we can be neighbors."

"That sounds like fun; I'll help you build it. Since you are leaving tomorrow morning, I'll prepare some food for your journey."

I thanked him and went to bed early. I was so exhausted from digging the whole day that I didn't even hear the monsters later that night; I just slept like a baby.

Thursday

I woke up early and headed out the door. I ran off into the direction whence I came. But this time, I decided to run at maximum speed rather than turtling around. I needed to make it there and have time to gather material.

I don't know how long the gathering process will take, so I thought I should give myself more time by traveling quickly.

I found that from sprinting all the time, it made me hungry very quickly. I took out the food that Bob packed me and tried his cooked salmon. It was delicious and immediately filled me with energy, so I kept on running.

In my haste, I wasn't really watching the ground. Out of nowhere, I tripped over a rock and went tumbling. I ended up in a small dirt hole that looked kind of familiar.

Wait a minute, I thought to myself, *this hole looks a little bit TOO familiar. Nooo!! It can't be! This hole is one of the poo holes I dug on Monday. EWWWW!!*

I had fallen in my own poo. This had to be some sort of epic fail. After crying a little bit, only a little bit, I dusted myself off and continued my journey. After a while, I ran into a group of sheep. They were very cute and fluffy, and I thought I could use some of that wool for something later.

I tried cutting some wool off, but it was difficult because I didn't have the right tool. Finally, I gave in and decided to slay the sheep in hopes that would drop some wool.

"Sorry, sheep, but your time has come," I said sadly.

"BaaaaAaAAaa…" was all the sheep said.

Thwack!! Thwack!!

BAAA!! BAaAaahhh!! Baaa....aaaaahh......aahhh......aa...

Thwack!! Thwack!!

My wooden sword was stained with blood. No more cute and fluffy sheep, but at least I got my wool. Also, I was able to gather some raw mutton pieces. I walked away and continued my journey, while feeling slightly guilty about the innocent sheep.

I arrived at the ghost town at a bit after noon. I was assuming the time because I saw that the sun was past its midpoint. There was not a person in sight, and the town was completely overrun by slime cubes.

I didn't want to fight them, so I snuck around the town gathering materials like wood, stone, and torches.

Before I knew it, I had already demolished nearly half the village. I had collected tons of materials, and I could finally now build a proper house for myself. It was a moment of happiness for me, but there was no time to celebrate.

Darkness was coming, so I headed off to the church to resume my old post. Instead of firing arrows into the darkness throughout the night, I chose to just rest and relax instead.

There was no point in trying to defeat the mobs here because I wouldn't be protecting anyone. I took a few moments to construct a bed for myself using the wool and wood I collected earlier. It was quite nice laying up on the rooftop looking at the stars, moon, and clouds. Now, if I could only get those zombies to shut up and let me go to sleep.

Friday

I woke up a bit late today, but it is okay, it is important to rest well
when tired. I resumed gathering materials until about noon, and then
I headed back to my new village. I wasn't looking forward to the
travel, but there was no choice.

After about five hours of sprinting, I finally arrived at the new
village. Everyone was happy to see me, and I showed them all the
cool materials I collected.

We decided to place the torches immediately because nighttime will
be here soon. I placed a few torches by the unfinished trench. I also
placed a couple near Bob's house because I wanted to build a house
near there.

Even though I was tired, there was still a lot of work to be done, so I
got to work building the foundations of my house. I worked
throughout the night putting my house together piece by piece. I
used both wooden and stone blocks.

The night was upon us now. I saw a few zombies fall into the unfinished trench. It was working! They couldn't get out. I just sat there, pointed my finger at them and laughed. But then a skeleton archer spotted me, so I hid behind a building before he could get a shot off. This was when I realized the folly of my trench. Though, it could stop zombies, it can't stop arrows.

I guess once the trench is done, the next part of upgrading the village's defense would be to build a wall right behind the trench. That would look so cool; the village would look like a castle or something.

While hiding behind the building, a few zombies saw me from the other side of the village. They started coming my way, so it was time to run back to Bob's and hide behind his iron door.

I got to Bob's house and banged on the door. "Bob! Let me in! It is Steve."

There was no answer.

Holy moly, where is Bob? If he doesn't open up, I'm gonna become zombie food soon, I thought to myself. Later on, I found out that Bob was, indeed, home; he was just an incredibly heavy sleeper.

The zombies were getting closer. I had no choice; I had to fight them. There were five zombies; now, normally this wouldn't be too big of a deal, but I had been working all day, so I was tired, hungry, and low on energy.

But it was kill or be killed, so I mustered up the last of my energy, drew out my wooden sword and swung away.

The zombies hit me a few times, but my leather tunic was able to absorb some of the damage. I was really low on health, but I had to keep fighting.

Thwack!! Thwack!! And Thwack some more!!

I yelled out my battle cry, "Die, you brain leeches!!"

One by one, the zombies fell, but more kept coming. I guess I was being too loud or something. They pushed me up against some random house, and my body slammed against the door.

Oh, no! I'm surrounded. There's nowhere left to run. I can't circle strafe myself out of this pinch, I thought, *I'm done for.*

At that moment when the outcome looked most bleak, the door behind me opened up. Cindy grabbed me, pulled me in the house, and shut the door behind her. She locked the door tight, and we both pushed up against the door to try to reinforce it. The zombies moaned and banged against the door.

The house shook, the wooden door creaked, we were both scared witless.

"What are we gonna do, Steve? What if they break through the door?" she asked in a frightened voice.

"D-don't worry, I-I can still fight," I replied shakily, while standing in a pool of my own blood.

"You're in no condition to fight! We need to think of something."

"Let's reinforce the door with something stronger," I told her, and then I reached into my bag and pulled out some stone blocks. "Here, this should do it."

We placed two stone blocks in a column behind the wooden door. We no longer had to hold the door, and the zombies wouldn't be able to break through stone even if they got through the door. We were finally able to relax a little.

"Thanks for saving me, Cindy."

"Of course, I couldn't let our village defender die on my doorstep, could I?"

I laughed. "I guess not. I need to recover my strength. Do you have anything to eat?"

"Here, have some bread. You shouldn't be so reckless out there, Steve."

"I know, sorry, I was overconfident. The zombies just swarmed me out of nowhere, and they just kept on coming," I replied while eating.

"Yeah, zombies tend to do that, ya know?"

"I'm gonna be more prepared next time. I'll craft some armor tonight, and then go to bed."

"Okay, great idea. I'll see you in the morning, Steve."

I worked late into the night to create a full set of leather armor out of the leather pieces I got from the cows the other day. I tried it on when I was done, and I have to say, I looked quite magnificent.

I also took this opportunity to craft some stone shovels to give to the villagers. I fell asleep shortly after.

Saturday

I got up bright and early today, so that I could get a head start on digging the trench. I felt much better after eating and resting and now am ready to face the new day. I gave all the volunteers stone shovels, and our work productivity skyrocketed. At this rate, we should be done in no time.

At about midday, Lisa the wise elder approached me.

"Steve, you are extremely passionate about defending our humble village. For that, I thank you," she said.

"I feel it is my duty to defend others. Please, no thanks are necessary," I replied unpretentiously.

"Good, good. If you are truly serious about protecting the village, perhaps you will be interested in taking these village upgrades a few steps further."

"What did you have in mind?" I asked curiously.

"Well, you see, our people have been blessed by a special type of guardian. This guardian comes to protect us only if our village is deemed worthy."

"Really? That is interesting! What makes a village worthy?" I asked inquisitively.

Lisa smiled because she enjoyed my enthusiasm. "For a village to be deemed worthy, the villagers must be happy and prosperous. They must have plentiful food, plentiful shelter, plentiful trades, just basically a life of abundance."

"I see…."

She continued to explain, "Once a village lives in abundance, it will grow in size. More buildings and homes will have to be built. Right now, we currently have nine villagers living here. If you can raise that number to about 16 villagers total, our magical guardian will appear and protect our village 24 hours a day."

"Okay, that sounds quite amazing, but it also sounds like a lot of work, like A LOT."

"Yes, indeed, you would have to build more farms, more homes, and collect and trade with the villagers to make them happy," she said.

"Uh, yeah, I don't know if I am capable of doing all that right away because that sounds like a lot of work…" I replied hesitatingly.

"I understand. Yes, the whole entire process could take months, maybe years. But the good news is that there is a way to build a guardian."

"Oh? Now that's something I could probably complete quickly."

"Ah, but it is kind of tricky. You see, you will require a huge amount of iron ingots, 36 to be precise. Also, you need to find a pumpkin, which seems to be extremely rare."

"Yikes, where am I going to find all of those items? I guess I could travel and dig around a bit."

"I'm sorry, I can't help you there, but your guess is as good as mine. I bid you good luck and farewell, Steve, defender of our village." She began to walk away.

"Yes, thank you Lisa, for your wisdom and guidance. I will put this knowledge to good use."

At around 4pm, we completed digging the trench around the entire village. We all cheered and everyone was happy. All of our hard work has produced this amazing defensive structure.

I told everyone about what happened last time at the other village. I told them how we celebrated too early and were overconfident, and then later the monsters broke through.

So, this time instead of partying right away, we decided to put the trench to the test first. We'll see how it will perform later tonight, and if it works well, we'll celebrate tomorrow morning. At about 6pm, everyone returned to their homes just like every other night.

I continued to work on my house next to Bob's. He came out and helped me a bit. We were about half way done with it until we started hearing zombies groan. After that, we both ran back into his house for cover.

As we waited the night out, we could hear the monsters in the distance, but never did they bang on our door as they usually do. I think that meant that the trench worked, but I wasn't sure.

I guess we'll have to wait until tomorrow morning to find out. We were both tired from working all day, so we just knocked out early.

Sunday

I was excited to wake up this morning. I couldn't wait to go see the trench, so I skipped breakfast and ran outside. I looked into the trench that we dug and found a bunch of zombies on fire.

I laughed and yelled, "Look, everyone! The zombies are all stuck down there, and the sunlight is killing them. Our plan worked!"

The villagers came over cautiously; they aren't too fond of being close to zombies. But when they saw that the zombies were stuck, they all cheered.

"Hooray! Steve has done it! Our champion is the best! This calls for celebration!" some of the villagers shouted.

The mayor came over to congratulate me. "Great job, son. You've done good for our village. Our people will be forever in your debt."

"It is no problem, sir. But there is still much work to do, and I'll get on it soon."

"Ah, good. This is why you are our champion," he replied, smiled and patted me on the back.

Everyone was happy and thankful for the village's new defense structure. They cooked and brought out tons of food for everyone to share. Bob decided to bake some goodies, and I smelled them from a mile away. He brought out cookies and cakes, which I devoured immediately.

My favorites were the double chocolate chip cookies. Coming in at second place would be the oatmeal raisin cookies. I just inhaled those treats; they didn't stand a chance. I felt kind of bad afterward because those cookies were supposed to be for everyone, but instead I ate them all by myself.

Good thing no one seemed to mind, that has to be the perk of being the village champion. However, I think some of the younger children were upset with me, though.

We celebrated throughout the day, and when the night came, no one rushed home. In fact, a few brave villagers stayed out to check out the night sky.

As for me, however, I was indoors designing my home and planning the next defensive upgrade. There was still much work to do, and I couldn't afford to slack off just yet. After all, a champion's work is never done.

I am happy with my new home and happy with my new neighbors. I will do my absolute best to protect them all. I will not let the past repeat itself in this new village. No, this time I am prepared. I will continue to learn, grow, and upgrade my equipment. I will be ready for whatever challenge comes next. The idea of having a guardian to protect the village sounds great, but the cost sounds extremely high. I will have to research and look into it more next week. Until then, see you later.

Can You Help Me Out?

Thanks for reading all the way through. I hope that you enjoyed this book. As a new writer, it is hard to get started; it is difficult to find an audience that wants to read my books. There are millions of books out there and sometimes it is super hard to find one specific book. But that's where you come in! You can help other readers find my books by leaving a simple review. It doesn't have to be a lengthy or well written review; it just has to be a few words and then click on the stars. It would take less than 5 minutes.

Seriously, that would help me so much, you don't even realize it. Every time I get a review, good or bad, it just fills me with motivation to keep on writing. It is a great feeling to know that somewhere out there, there are people who actually enjoy reading my books. Anyway, I would super appreciate it, thanks.

If you see new books from me in the future, you will know that I wrote them because of your support. Thank you for supporting my work.

Special thanks again to previous readers and reviewers. Thank you for encouraging me to keep writing. I'll do my best to provide high quality books for you all.

My Other Books

Check Out My Author Page
Steve the Noob

My Awesome List of Favorite

Readers and Reviewers

W. shi "Jenn"

K.K "mysweetdees"

Mikail

WarCenturion

Stephanie Linn

Thank you so much for your support. You guys and girls rock!!

Jewel Shine

Minoscreeperslayer

RainbowCreeper

Sang Chul Choi

Misahti

Panisara W.

Astro Cat

AthanEnder

betsy

akaherobrine

James

Xaxier Edwards

leann xiao

Awesomeguy27

IsaBear556

Emma Hogan

Brandon Kim

Venu Gopal

Kathy

Yuan Cui

Sreekant Gottimukkala

Emma

Kayla Dingo

ZombieCupcake

Ding Zhou

Alex

spark527

Gator

Nick

devlin

Grant

MeowLord

Ducky MooMoo

Minecarft Book Girl

Jax/Blaze7381

Steve

Toni

Jane

Jacob

PigMaster4000

Skyler

Kayla Ding

Kareem

shard

Cole

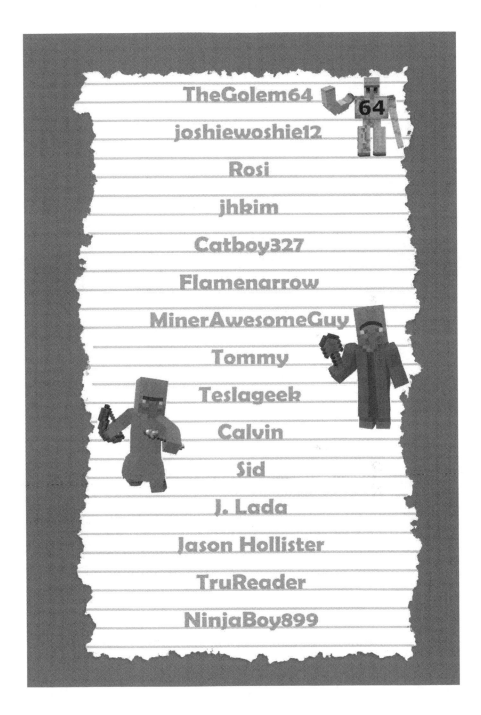

TheGolem64

joshiewoshie12

Rosi

jhkim

Catboy327

Flamenarrow

MinerAwesomeGuy

Tommy

Teslageek

Calvin

Sid

J. Lada

Jason Hollister

TruReader

NinjaBoy899

Onjl

owlfeatherr

Dude89

Zachary Ln

haminal77

No One In Particular

Kate B.

Lynn Sims

Da Lover of Da Cats

love it

Michael Sonn

M. Hooper

dayli ward

cameron

Calvin

john

shadow

matthkol

SkyMinecraft

Wendy

BobTheCow8274/Waylon

MarlaR

boi15

HappyPierceP

W

vighnesh

xNoobEvilBanana

TheJediMaster28

Lawton E. Paddock

Hyped Reviewer

JumpSlime

Ronan Bruno

Rainbow Cat 7562

Yan Guo

diamond girl

SkylarHearts

Joowon hwang

Dirt

Lucifer Hunt

Austyn

#1sonicfan

MineFox

Louis

JenaLuv & Boogie

nerf boy

kall20

Power

S.U.P.E.R. X.P.E.R. - -

TheRealLukester

yong ye

Cfee

PlasmaGamerYT/InvolateMoss22

LittleCrafter11

Nickelworld123

Snakebeast7865

Lora Bean

m78

Paul 14689

Alpha44

Xeevee

AlabasterFoil32

Nexon1

ExplodingEmerald

joowon/superxper178

Ethan

coolshinwon07

Xx_Gameknight_xX- Conor

Charles Wen

LegoWarrior70

Foxfire

Thane

dm

Coolman100

CommanderBiffle

Reagan

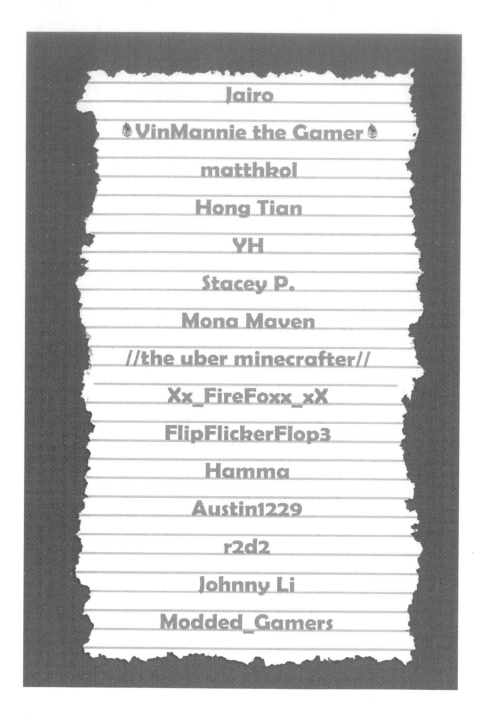

Jairo

🔥VinMannie the Gamer🔥

matthkol

Hong Tian

YH

Stacey P.

Mona Maven

//the uber minecrafter//

Xx_FireFoxx_xX

FlipFlickerFlop3

Hamma

Austin1229

r2d2

Johnny Li

Modded_Gamers

EmeraldGolem

Christo and Jon

adorkable cow

Ruffarian01

PaintyMcgee

Matthew

Daisy Cat

Wyatt

Windavour

Creepersko

BM

Vighnesh Anoop

PlyingMinotaur1

Lunalalordlol

EnderDragon

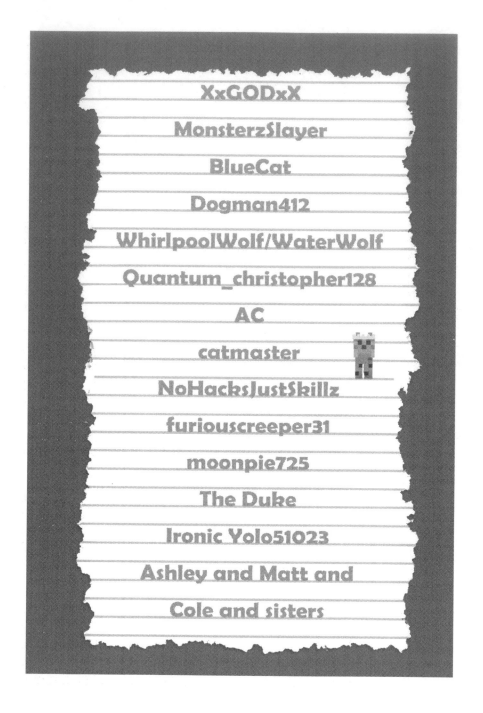

XxGODxX

MonsterzSlayer

BlueCat

Dogman412

WhirlpoolWolf/WaterWolf

Quantum_christopher128

AC

catmaster

NoHacksJustSkillz

furiouscreeper31

moonpie725

The Duke

Ironic Yolo51023

Ashley and Matt and

Cole and sisters

ilovedragons1

Sugary_Gamer

HoopeCade000

Sy

Mr. Gamer

wenlan

EPICSNIPEZ3355

flame555

Endercreeper

Meh Meh

Mr_Rainboww

hate it

EnderBlaze125

Cuno

posh shotfox

Lucky Buster

Bailey

molloni & BlookittiePC

JayD24

E. Harris

Camden

Commander Twinkles

Kelly Greene

Foodiej

Andrew

LudwigVonKoopa

WitherSkelebone

dadirtdatsings

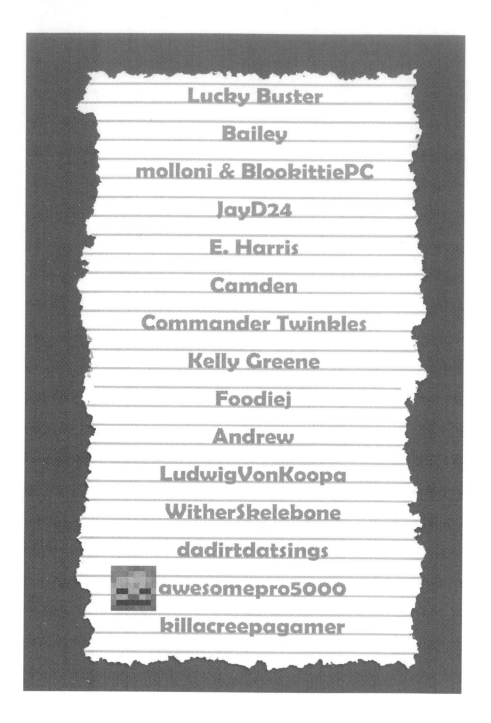 awesomepro5000

killacreepagamer

Michel

ImTooLazyToThinkOfAName

tuckster7

QuaxyGaming

quackz123

esther

cool bro64

the gaming creeper

zombie slayer 2001#%~

moonpie725

ItsRemarks

Sydney

NoHaxJustSkillz

Arni

Mr. Gamer

Kaptain kitkat

K.M.T.

pacman2022

Ava

zombieguy304

nitroblock

drgody gamer

jackie howard

patrick d albrecht

Tom

killian

The Phenox

pug

Quackz123

Expl0d1ngK1w1

Darrow

Rezno

TheEntity303

Ashton

EJO

Chase

IzzMan24

molloni & BlookittiePC

XxSNIPERPROxX

Uphillkookoo132

Monyface

pikachu_99999

Effie

Kool Kids

Johnny

Slimehead1212

DanyaAK

Riptide91837

KlunderTale

AG

Blaise

Ruffarian

B-dwag

Phantom Dilbert

Tiffany

Bon

MCplayer101

Timmy70574

Kevin

Braydenfree123

Bolt

Lan

Justanothergame

A Reader of Many Things

XxProBloxxerXx

TubbyMcWilson

NutNutty

Jude164

Avery

diamondgirl1615

RealPixelPl

Michael Sonn

Dark realmer

 ME NO LIKE GAVY

Laila

MysteryRanger

boi15

ASHTON SALTOU

walrush2oball

Fireskrull

Luca (aka Nologout)

ILIKEZMEHWAFFLEZ

Knight

bespiked101

beverly upshaw

Spartan Lord

UltimateSword5

catmaster

Kaming

RealPixelPI

iron killer 001

XAncientNinjaX(Ninja Jack)

Elijah LeFavour

darkflame

Peyton the gladiator

Eva

survivor

Mary

claire creeper

A DOG

Amit

Deso333

Zorgon

w

Sutter

The mighty steve

clockman80

Hamster girl

Lord Ender

CryingGahst112

Searcher

Sans Er

Sparkle girl

happy squid 😄😄😄😄😄😄

LunarComete

danny117

Stampy Fox

Meredith

TheRogue35

Tubby

cottoncandy

HeroGamer

LazyGhost

Carlos the musketeer

agent cat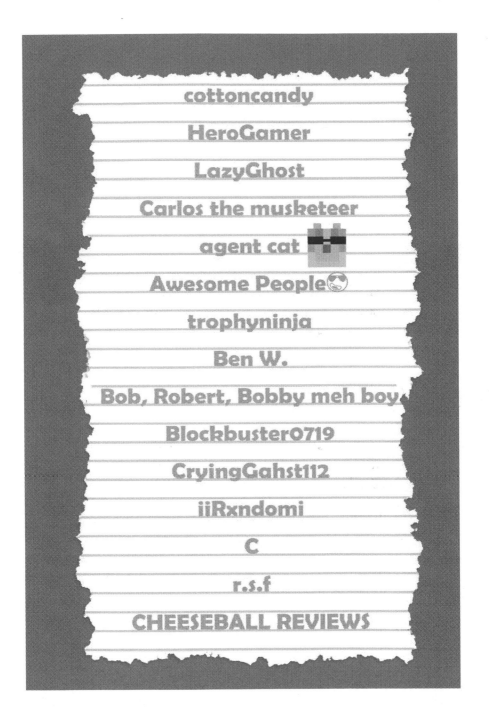

Awesome People

trophyninja

Ben W.

Bob, Robert, Bobby meh boy

Blockbuster0719

CryingGahst112

iiRxndomi

C

r.s.f

CHEESEBALL REVIEWS

boi the builder

LSY

boxyfox

JayD24

Herobrine

da beast

UltimateSword5

Uphillkookoo132

Richardawesome

CheckerMaster

rainbow dog

Mathaniel

agent blacksmith bob

Arctic54

Beast the Guy

Awesomeness47

ZE MINECRAFT FAN

Zach

MobMaster937

Cole the torch

glassesgamergirlYT

JaCrazygamex

Machine60

Jacob

yan zhu

callum

TglgPlayz

L@z¥Gho§t

ninjago cat awsome guy

HyruleLegend

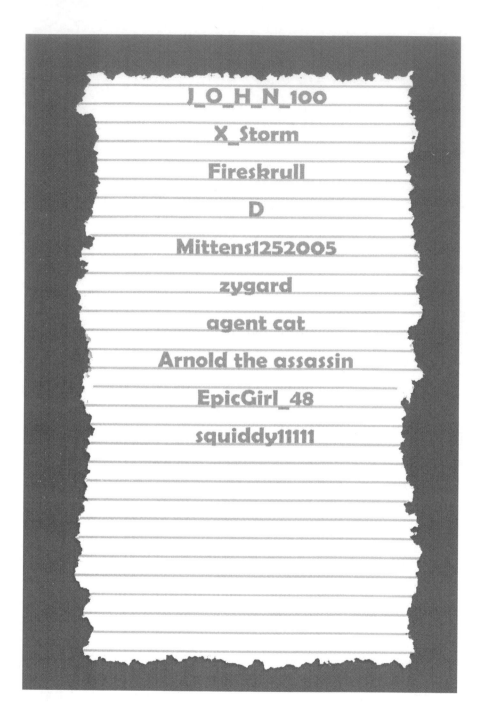

J_O_H_N_100

X_Storm

Fireskrull

D

Mittens1252005

zygard

agent cat

Arnold the assassin

EpicGirl_48

squiddy11111

Made in the USA
San Bernardino, CA
06 November 2017